THE COMFORT ZONE

LILLENAS DRAMA

THE COMFORT ZONE

11 Sketches
to Challenge and
Encourage the Christian Faith

by Chuck Neighbors

author of **The What Would Jesus Do? Playbook**

Lillenas PUBLISHING COMPANY

KANSAS CITY, MO 64141

Questions? Please write or call:
    Lillenas Publishing Company
    Drama Resources
    P.O. Box 419527
    Kansas City, MO 64141
    Phone: 816-931-1900 ● Fax: 816-412-8390
    E-mail: drama@lillenas.com
    Web: www.lillenas.com/drama

Cover art by Michael Walsh

Dedication

To my wife, Lorie, and my boys, Jonathan, Ryan, and Liam.
You make my life complete!

Preface

The "comfort zone." What comes to your mind when you hear those words? Is it a good thing or a bad thing?

I guess it depends.

For me, when I am doing something that is outside my area of expertise, like, say, almost anything to do with home improvement projects, I'm outside my comfort zone. And according to my wife it needs to stay that way. Just let me mention tackling some project that involves a power tool and she is pulling out the phone book to call the professionals. It's OK . . . I know where my gifts are, and Home Depot is not going to get wealthy off of people like me.

Some people have comfort zones in places that they probably shouldn't. Like my wife and the mall. You ask me, she is way too comfortable there. While she is in her comfort zone spending our hard-earned cash, I am forced outside my comfort zone when the bills come in. It makes me very uncomfortable to spend money on women's shoes. Can somebody explain to me what it is with women and shoes?

Then there are those comfort zones that are a good thing. Things like spending quality time with family and friends. Doing things you enjoy that fall in your area of interest or expertise; be they things like teaching, coaching, cooking, and for some even using power tools.

When you go in for surgery, it is reassuring to know that the operating room is a comfort zone for your doctor. (But not too comfortable. It's not a good sign if CNN is playing on the monitor.)

I have another comfort zone. It is a big blue recliner in front of our TV. Put me there and nothing gets done that needs doing.

Ah, yes, doing things that need to get done . . . Sometimes we avoid doing things we know we should because they fall outside our comfort zone, and they are easy to avoid for that very reason. But just because something is outside our comfort zone, is it right to avoid it altogether?

Some people don't go to church because it makes them uncomfortable. I am hesitant to go to certain group events because being around a bunch of strangers makes me uncomfortable—my wife's company Christmas party, for example.

This book contains a play called "The Comfort Zone." It is about a family trying to come to terms with the worship styles that exist in our culture today. You see, there's this church in town that crowds their comfort zone. Doing something, anything, differently can cause a ripple in our comfort zone. One of the things that makes this family uncomfortable is the fact that this church does drama on a regular basis. (I'll bet you were wondering when I was going to get around to talking about drama!)

Drama can do that rather well. It can be uncomfortable to see ourselves portrayed on the stage. It can make us laugh and cry, both things that can make people uncomfortable (especially the crying). Sometimes it contains so much truth that it can unsettle an entire audience—very uncomfortable, but it can be a very good thing! The very concepts of change and growth are not comfortable thoughts, but are necessary and good nonetheless.

So I offer up this collection of scripts to challenge and encourage, to make you laugh, cry, and maybe squirm. May you find yourself in your comfort zone as you perform them. May you prod some people out of their comfort zones as they experience them!

Ten thousand blessings on you!

Chuck Neighbors

Contents

The Comfort Zone

Themes: Relevancy of the church, traditional vs. contemporary worship, accepting change

Scripture: Mark 9:38-41

Cast:

MOM: *a traditional mom*
DAD: *a traditional dad*
TERRI: *their daughter, a typical teenager*

Props:

Assorted makeup and bathroom items (e.g., deodorant, aftershave, comb, hand soap, tissue)
A man's tie and sport coat
Bible

Running Time: 6 minutes

(A traditional family home. To be even more specific, the master bathroom of a traditional family home. There is a small table to represent a bathroom counter DSC and a chair USR that also serves to mark the entrance to the bathroom from the master bedroom. Characters will face the audience as if they are looking in the bathroom mirror. It is Sunday morning and the family is preparing to go to church. As the scene opens, TERRI is putting the finishing touches on her hair, a ponytail straight up on top or something nontraditional that MOM will not approve of. She is dressed in jeans and a T-shirt [or clothing that reflects the latest fad]. MOM enters the bathroom to do her makeup, which she will work on throughout the scene. MOM is dressed in her Sunday best dress or blouse and skirt. Note: Be sure to practice the bits of business in the mirror. A great deal of humor can be derived from accurately depicting the everyday things we do in front of a mirror!)

MOM: Terri, what are you doing in here? Why aren't you in the other bathroom?

TERRI: Dad is in there. *(A knowing look)* With the Sunday paper.

MOM: Oh *(understanding)*, then he'll be there for a while. I wish he wouldn't do that. Well *(redoing TERRI's hair)*, we have to leave for church in 15 minutes. You had better hurry and get dressed.

TERRI: I am dressed, Mom.

MOM: I mean for church.

TERRI: I know what you mean. I'm dressed.

11

MOM: I beg your pardon!? You are not wearing that. This is church we are going to, not some rock concert.

TERRI: But, Mom, Cheryl wears clothes like this to her church. Why can't I dress the way I want at our church?

MOM: Because this is our church, not Cheryl's. Besides, what would people say if they saw you dressed that way?

TERRI: Who cares. (*Looking at the dress* MOM *has on*) Mom, nobody my age wears those kinda dresses anymore. (*Referring to her own clothes now*) This is who I am.

MOM: Not this morning. Become somebody else today. Go change your clothes.

TERRI: I thought you said God accepts us the way we are.

MOM: He does. But not at church. I mean, church is about people, not about . . . (*Oops, catches herself about to say something she knows is not right.*) Never mind. You are not wearing that to church. Now go change.

TERRI: I wish I could go to Cheryl's church. (*She exits just as* DAD *enters in time to hear her last line. He crosses to the chair where his tie and sport coat are laid out.*)

DAD: What's this about Cheryl's church? (*Moves in front of mirror to start working with his tie. He will then continue with other business such as deodorant, aftershave, combing hair . . .*)

MOM: Did you see the way she was dressed? She actually thought she could get away with wearing that to church.

DAD (*dismissing the whole thing with one word*): Kids. What does that have to do with Cheryl's church?

MOM: Oh, according to her, Cheryl is allowed to dress that way for church. They go to that church on Hollings Street, you know, the one that doesn't look like a church.

DAD: Oh, that one. Tim Anderson, from work, goes there. From what I understand, not only does it not look like a church, but they don't act much like a church either.

MOM: What do you mean?

DAD: Well, to begin with, there is the music. Evidently they don't have a choir and they don't use hymnals.

TERRI (*from offstage*): Mom, have you seen my Steven Curtis Chapman CD?

MOM: What, dear? (*Back to* DAD) What do they do? They have music, don't they?

DAD: Yes, in fact he said they sing a lot, but mostly just choruses, and according to Tim, it's very, uh . . . what was his word . . . contemporary. It is all that electric stuff—guitars, synthesizers, and get this—drums!

MOM: Drums! Sounds like rock to me. *(Tsk, tsk)* And at church!

TERRI *(offstage, impatiently)*: Mom! Where is my Steven Curtis Chapman CD?!

MOM *(calling out)*: It's in the car, Terri. I borrowed your Jars of Clay CD too. They should be in the CD case, along with my Elton John collection. *(Back to the conversation)* If you ask me, that kind of music doesn't belong in church.

DAD: I agree. Oh, another thing Tim was saying was that they have what he called a "drama ministry," and they sometimes perform these "plays" on Sunday morning as a part of the church service.

MOM: You're kidding! Drama during church. The church is a place of worship, not entertainment. Sounds to me like this church has its priorities mixed up. We get so much entertainment these days anyway. Sunday ought to be different.

DAD: Speaking of entertainment. I was just checking the paper for show times for *[insert current movie]*.

MOM *(accusing)*: In the bathroom.

DAD: In the bathroom. *(Shrugs, "so what")* If we want to catch the cheaper matinee today, we will have to hurry out after church. Don't stand and gab like you usually do.

MOM: Well, I only see these people once a week. I have to be polite. Some of them are our friends, you know.

DAD: Yeah, I guess so . . . Not close ones, though . . . You know, Tim actually has a group from the church come to his house every Thursday night. What a hassle that would be!

MOM: Why? What do they do?

DAD: Got me. A study of some kind, I think.

MOM: Strange. They must be fanatics or something. Anyway, I will hurry today. I just hope Rev. Borland doesn't go "over" again like he did last week.

DAD: He does drone on sometimes, doesn't he?

MOM: How would you know? You fall asleep after the first hymn and don't wake up until the final "amen."

DAD: That is not true and you know it. They take the offering just before the sermon and you always jab me in the ribs just before the plate goes by. Besides, Sunday is a day of rest after all, and what better place to rest than at the house of the Lord!

MOM: I suppose they don't even have a sermon at that other church. . . . You'd probably like that part.

DAD: No, I am comfortable where we are. And they do have a sermon. According to Tim, it is more of a "teaching time" than a sermon. Evidently the pastor doesn't even use a pulpit and usually sits on a stool. Tim says he has only heard him shout once, and that was when he somehow got an electrical shock from the microphone.

MOM: Doesn't sound like a church at all to me. Who would go to such a church?

DAD: Well, some people must. Tim says they have doubled in size in the last year alone.

MOM: Really? And our church seems to be dwindling. I wonder why? *(Checks her watch)* Well, we better go or we will be late. You know how much I hate having to sit in the front.

DAD: Right. *(Shouting)* Terri, are you ready? Let's go! *(Putting on his jacket)*

TERRI *(enters in a dress that resembles her mother's, wearing a Walkman and singing Steve Curtis Chapman's "Dive" or some other popular contemporary Christian tune; said without enthusiasm):* Yeah, I'm ready.

DAD: Good, I'll get the car started. *(Exits, followed by TERRI)*

MOM: I'll be right out. *(Starts humming same tune TERRI was singing, picks up her Bible, and practices a pious look in the mirror. She then starts singing "Amazing Grace" as she exits.)*

The end

Discussion starters:

1. How would you describe this family's attitudes toward church and worship?

2. Is there anything wrong with the concept of church being a "place of entertainment"?

3. Are there elements of worship in your church that challenge your own "comfort zone"?

How to Catch a Fish

Themes: Lifestyle evangelism, relationships, communication

Scripture: 1 Corinthians 9:19-23

Cast:

BILL: *a Christian and a reluctant participant in this "evangelism thing"; a likeable guy, down-to-earth*

CAROL: *an overzealous Christian and an eager participant in this "evangelism thing"; tries too hard—does a good job at saying the wrong thing; married to Bill*

WAITRESS: *the observant and helpful type*

ZACH: *a good person, likable and decent but not a Christian; a good prospect for Bill and Carol*

SUSAN: *a good person, likable but stressed; not a Christian; Carol's prey; married to Zach*

Props:
A tablecloth
Cloth napkins
Flower or candle centerpiece
Restaurant menus
A cigarette
Ashtray
Four glasses of water
Serving tray
Money for tip

Running Time: 15 minutes

Note: This play is in two scenes, however the first scene can be done by itself, if desired. The second scene works well as a "epilogue," if the play is used in conjunction with a sermon.

Scene I

(A nice restaurant. There is a table for four DS just right of CS. US just left of center is a rostrum for reservations. BILL and CAROL MURPHY enter first. BILL looks around and then comes back to CAROL.)

BILL: Well, I don't see them. We must have beat them here.

CAROL: We are a few minutes early. They will probably be along any minute. Now remember why we are doing this. We are supposed to be building relationships so that . . .

BILL: Yeah, yeah, I know. Lifestyle evangelism. I hate that word—evangelism. I would rather use enthusiasm. Lifestyle enthusiasm.

CAROL: What is wrong with evangelism?

BILL: Nothing wrong with it, I guess. I mean, it needs to be done. But every time I hear the word I get visions of some televangelist yelling at people, telling them they are going to burn in hell. It is so negative, you know. Enthusiasm is a better word, at least for me. I mean, I am glad that I'm a Christian.

CAROL: Oh, Bill. It simply means sharing your faith with others. Let your "light shine," you know.

BILL: Yeah, well, I'll try. But this idea is making my bulb rather dim, if you know what I mean. I'm not sure I understand exactly what we are supposed to do. Can't we just have dinner with our new friends—no hidden agenda?

CAROL: Just be friendly and look for every opportunity to share your faith.

BILL: Every opportunity? Now that sounds like evangelism. I thought the idea was to build relationships, not preach.

CAROL: You don't have to preach, dear. We'll let the pastor do that part. But try to steer the conversation toward our faith. We have made good progress with the Watsons. The fact that they came to church with us last Sunday was a good indication that they are searching. Tonight could be the night!

BILL: The night for what?

CAROL: You know. The night that they get saved.

BILL: Saved! *(Hates that word too)* Tonight! . . . Carol, you're scaring me.

WAITRESS *(coming from other side of the stage):* Good evening. Just the two of you?

BILL: No, another couple is joining us. There'll be four.

WAITRESS: Smoking or nonsmoking?

CAROL: Nonsmoking.

BILL: Wait, Carol. Zach smokes. I'm not sure about Susan.

CAROL: Bill, I can't stand sitting in smoking. Besides, what if someone we know sees us? They might think we smoke. What would that do to our witness?

BILL: You have got to be kidding me.

CAROL: I am not. *(To* WAITRESS*)* Nonsmoking, please.

WAITRESS: Follow me.

BILL (*muttering*): I thought the idea was to build relationships.

CAROL: What does sitting in smoking have to do with building relationships?

BILL: Never mind. (*They both sit.*)

WAITRESS: Tonight we are offering a complimentary glass of champagne. Could I bring you a glass while you wait for your friends?

(*Together*)

BILL: Yes, please.

CAROL: No, thank you.

CAROL (*startled*): Bill, you don't drink. What are you doing?

BILL (*to* WAITRESS): Uh, never mind, two waters, please. (WAITRESS *leaves.*) Carol, I thought I would try a glass of champagne with my meal. That way if Zach or Carol drink it would make them feel more comfortable. Remember "relationships." One glass of champagne with a meal is not a problem for me. And besides—it's free!

CAROL: I can't believe you. You should know better . . .

(BILL *and* CAROL *fade into quiet discussion as* ZACH *and* SUSAN WATSON *enter near the rostrum.* ZACH *has a cigarette in his mouth.*)

ZACH: I think that's them over there.

SUSAN: Yes, that's them.

ZACH (*an arm around her*): Are you OK? I know you have had a rough day with the kids and all. I hope you can have a good time tonight.

SUSAN: I'll be fine, after a glass of wine. I enjoy the Murphys, as long as Carol doesn't corner me about her church stuff again. If she pesters me about coming to that women's Bible study one more time, I think I'll cry.

ZACH: I'll try to steer the conversation away from there. It's important to her, though.

SUSAN: Oh, I know. And I really did enjoy going to church with them. It was not at all what I expected. But Carol keeps bringing it up at every turn; it's like she is out to recruit me or something. It gets to be a bit much after awhile.

ZACH: That's too bad. Bill is much more down-to-earth. I think I may have finally found a guy in this town that I can relate to.

WAITRESS: Good evening. Smoking or nonsmoking?

ZACH (*looking toward the* MURPHYS, *a bit of a grimace*): It looks like nonsmoking tonight. We are with that couple over there. (*Puts out cigarette*)

WAITRESS *(a knowing smile about the smoking)*: Ah, yes, right this way.

(BILL *and* CAROL *are still in discussion about the champagne, don't see* WATSONS *approaching.* WATSONS *overhear their last comments.*)

BILL: . . . and anyway, Jesus drank wine.

CAROL: You are not having any. Anyway it wasn't real wine. It was grape juice and . . . *(Looks up)* Hi, Susan, Zach.

BILL *(standing, shakes hands)*: Hello, you two. Is this table OK?

SUSAN: Well, actually . . . *(A look at* ZACH, *knows he would rather sit in smoking.)*

ZACH *(quickly)*: Fine, Bill. Just fine.

WAITRESS *(handing out menus)*: We are offering a complimentary glass of champagne tonight. Can I bring you one?

SUSAN *(she could use one)*: That sounds . . .

ZACH *(a look at* SUSAN, *insightfully)*: Uh, I think a couple of waters will do it tonight. (WAITRESS *exits.*)

CAROL: Oh good, you don't drink. Did you know a lot of people think that Jesus drank wine? But I was just explaining to Bill that it wasn't really wine, it was juice. Did you know that? (BILL *looks at* CAROL—*can't believe she is saying this.*)

SUSAN: Uh, no, I didn't, Carol.

CAROL: Oh, that's OK. But you know there is so much to learn when you get involved in a good Bible study. You know that group I was telling you about? We meet on Wednesday mornings and . . .

ZACH *(rescuing* SUSAN)*: So, did you have any trouble finding this place? You seem to have beat us.

(WAITRESS *delivers water during following dialogue.*)

BILL: Not at all, good directions. It is really nice. I'm glad you invited us.

ZACH: The food is excellent. Especially the seafood. Do you like seafood?

BILL: I love it.

CAROL: Oh, me too.

SUSAN: Oh, good. Zach and I come here at least once a month. We think it's the best place in town.

CAROL: Say, speaking of the best place in town, I have been meaning to ask you all week—what did you think of church last Sunday?

SUSAN: We really enjoyed it, Carol. Thank you again for inviting us.

ZACH: Yes, thank you both. We wouldn't mind going again sometime.

CAROL (*a look of triumph at* BILL): That's great. How about tomorrow morning?

ZACH: Uh, I'm sorry, but I have an employee golf tournament.

CAROL: Well, they shouldn't schedule those things on a Sunday.

SUSAN: Why?

CAROL: Because it is the Lord's day.

SUSAN: Oh.

CAROL: What about you, Susan? Would you like to come with us? We could pick you up.

SUSAN: Oh, that is very kind of you. But I don't think so. I have had a very rough week and, if the kids will let me, I think I will try to sleep in the morning.

BILL: Oh sure, we understand, Susan. Some other time.

CAROL (*not giving up that easily*): Are you sure? Say, we could pick up the kids and take them to Sunday school. You could sleep in and then come to second service.

ZACH: Thanks, Carol, but the kids are being picked up by their grandparents at 11:00 in the morning. It won't work this week.

CAROL: Oh, well, maybe the week after next.

ZACH (*flatly*): Maybe.

WAITRESS (*coming back*): Well, are you folks ready to order? There is a special—not on the menu—salmon steak grilled in a honey mustard sauce and served with baby red potatoes, stir-fried vegetables, and garden salad with house dressing.

ZACH (*to everybody*): That's very good! We've had it before.

SUSAN: I'll have that.

CAROL: Me too.

BILL: Make it three.

ZACH: Well, it is unanimous then. Four specials!

WAITRESS: Well, that certainly was easy. Anything else to drink?

BILL: Just more water for us.

ZACH: More water would be fine. (WAITRESS *exits.*)

BILL: So you like seafood. Do you ever do any fishing?

ZACH: Yes! I love fishing. You?

BILL: You bet! Especially deep-sea fishing.

ZACH: Oh yes! There is nothing like it.

BILL: Last fall I caught a 41-pound chinook salmon in the mouth of the Columbia River. What an experience!

CAROL: Did you know that many of the disciples were fishermen?

(BILL *and* ZACH *both look at her as if to say "where did that come from?"*)

ZACH: Disciples?

CAROL: The disciples of Jesus.

ZACH: Oh.

CAROL: There are actually a lot of good fishing stories in the Bible. Right, Bill?

BILL: Uh, yeah, right, Carol. Anyway, we should go fishing together sometime, Zach!

ZACH: I'd love it! (*Looks toward* SUSAN, *who is still looking gloomy; reaches over and touches her*) You doing OK?

SUSAN: I'll be all right. Thanks.

ZACH: She has had a rough week. The kids have been particularly trying this week and today especially.

CAROL: Oh, I'm sorry. I know how that can be.

SUSAN: It started on Monday when the baby got sick in the middle of the night. Then it rained on Tuesday and all three of the kids and me were cooped up in the house all day. I thought I would go nuts, and then . . .

CAROL (*seizes her chance*): Have you read any of James Dobson's books? He is a Christian psychologist. He has a radio program on every day that is really helpful. It might help you with your problems. It would be really good if you could come to our Bible study group on Wednesday mornings. They have a children's program that runs at the same time so you don't have to worry about a sitter and . . .

SUSAN (*tension is building; she is trying to be pleasant but needs to escape*): Excuse me. I need to visit the little girl's room. (*Gets up*)

CAROL: I'll come with you.

SUSAN: No! . . . uh, that's all right. Really.

CAROL (*oblivious*): No, I insist. (*They exit.*)

ZACH (*awkward pause*): Say, while they are gone, would you mind if I stepped out for a smoke?

BILL: No, not at all. I'll come with you and tell you more about that fish I caught. We went out real early and the water was quite choppy, 10 foot swells, I lost my breakfast after about 20 minutes . . . (*They exit.*)

Scene II

(*Same as Scene I. The couples have finished eating and are getting to their feet.* ZACH *has just paid the bill.*)

BILL: Well, Zach and Susan, thank you for inviting us to have dinner with you. I really enjoyed it.

ZACH: It was our pleasure.

CAROL: Yes, I enjoyed it too. Susan, I will give you a call next week about coming to church. I'll be praying for you.

SUSAN (*not enthusiastically, can't wait to leave*): Great.

BILL: Listen, we'll take care of the tip.

ZACH: Are you sure?

BILL: Absolutely. It's the least we can do since you picked up the tab.

ZACH: Well, thank you. We'll see you later.

BILL: Good night! I'll get back to you about that fishing trip. Oh, and good luck in the golf tournament tomorrow.

ZACH: Thanks! Good night, Bill, Carol.

CAROL: Good night, Susan.

SUSAN: Good night, Carol.

(ZACH *and* SUSAN *exit.* BILL *and* CAROL *hang back at the table to leave tip.*)

CAROL: Well that went well, didn't it? I think I gave Susan some things to think about. How did you think it went with Zach?

(BILL *gives her a look that says it all. A sort of, "I don't know you—I can't believe you did what you did—and I especially can't believe that you think what you did was good!" look.*)

CAROL (*her first moment of perception that evening*): What? (BILL *just shakes his head.*) What? (*He exits; she is close behind.*) Bill, what is wrong? Bill?

The end

Discussion starters:

1. What is wrong with Carol's approach to evangelism?

2. Give examples of how this scene could have be played with a positive outcome?

3. Discuss your own fears (or lack of fear) in the area of evangelism?

Sprinkled, Dunked, or Left Out in the Rain

Themes: Tolerance, understanding, evangelism, baptism

Scripture: Colossians 2:6-23

Cast:
ANN: *a Christian, the evangelical, zealous kind*
JILL: *a non-Christian but open and seeking*
BARB: *another Christian, but from a different "camp" than Ann*

Props:
Three coffee cups
Box of doughnuts
2 small invitation cards in envelopes

Running Time: 6 minutes

(The lunchroom of a large business. It's coffee break time on Friday. JILL *is seated at a table, coffee and doughnuts at hand, when* ANN *enters.)*

ANN: T.G.I.F! I love Fridays. I live for the weekends. I can't wait! *(Sits)* Oh good, you saved me a cake doughnut. I love to dunk them in my coffee.

JILL: Do you have plans?

ANN: Mega! Bill and I are going out on a real date tonight. No kids, no talk about work, just the two of us at a nice restaurant. Then tomorrow our Young Married Class from church is having a barbecue at Wilson Park. Then there's church on Sunday. It'll be a busy weekend—but I love it.

JILL: You are very involved in your church, aren't you?

ANN: Yes, I am. My faith, Christianity, is very important to me—us—our family.

JILL: Tell me more about this Young Married Class. What is it? What do you study? Marriage? Do you have to be young . . . ?

ANN *(laughs):* Yes and no. Perhaps it is not a very good name. Not very original, I guess. It is just a name for married couples in the twenty- to thirty-something age bracket. You and Eric qualify. We do study marriage sometimes, but other times we study anything from books of the Bible to relevant social issues. Why don't you guys join us tomorrow at the barbecue . . . get to know some of the people. You'd really like them. Or come to church with us on Sunday.

JILL: But we aren't Christians. I don't think we would fit in.

ANN: Sure you would. That doesn't matter. Hey, we accept you the way you are. Give it a try. Check us out!

JILL: Sounds tempting. Eric and I really don't have anything "extra" in our lives—other than work. We need something . . . I'm feeling a little . . .

BARB (comes bouncing in): Hi, Jill. Hi, Ann. How goes it?

JILL: Not bad, I guess.

ANN: Great! It is Friday, after all. The "weekend" awaits us.

BARB: Could you pass me the doughnut with sprinkles? (JILL does.) Thanks. This is an exciting weekend for us. In fact, Jim and I want to give you each one of these. (Hands them each a small envelope) Our little Emily is being baptized this Sunday at church. (Gushing a bit) We would be thrilled if you could both come—be a part of it.

JILL: Being baptized? I have heard about that. What is . . . ?

(During the following dialogue, JILL feels left out, as if she is listening to a foreign language.)

ANN (ignoring JILL): I'm sorry, Barb, but we don't agree with that. Our church teaches believer's baptism.

BARB (tensing up): Yes, I know they do, Ann. I'm not asking you to agree with anything. I simply invited you to come to the service.

ANN: But if we did, it would be endorsing something we feel is wrong.

BARB: Wrong?! I don't believe this. It is one thing to say that you don't agree. I mean, I am open-minded enough to, as they say, "agree to disagree," but to say something is wrong just because you don't agree?!

ANN: That is part of the problem with you and your church. You are too "open-minded," if you ask me.

BARB: That's not true! But at least we don't think we have a corner on the truth like yours does.

JILL (to BARB, trying to understand): Excuse me, but isn't your church a Christian church?

BARB (defensive, thinks that is rather obvious): Well, of course.

ANN: Well, they say that. But they don't believe the Bible.

BARB: I beg your pardon! We most certainly do!

ANN (*a challenge*): Chapter and verse, where does it say that you should baptize babies?

BARB: Back at you! Chapter and verse, where does it say that you shouldn't?

ANN (*to* JILL): Their church teaches that you have to be sprinkled.

JILL (*confused*): Sprinkled?

BARB (*to* JILL): Can you believe that they actually have a big bathtub in their church that they dunk you in.

JILL (*more confused*): Dunk?

ANN: That's the way Jesus was baptized!

JILL: In a bathtub?

ANN: It's not a bathtub. I mean, He was immersed. You know.

JILL (*has no idea*): Oh . . .

BARB: That is a matter of interpretation.

ANN: Oh, here we go again. Anytime you liberals don't want to accept what the Bible says, you give us that "interpretation" line.

BARB: You fundamentalists are all the same. You are such hypocrites. You say you believe every jot and tittle—but I notice that you cut your hair. Now what did Paul say about that?

ANN: That was a part of the culture!

BARB (*sarcastically*): Isn't that a matter of interpretation?

(JILL *is getting up to leave.*)

BARB: Wait, Jill. It is obvious that Ann won't be coming on Sunday, but what about you? Can we count on you to be there?

ANN: I'm sorry, Barb, but Jill is coming to church with me on Sunday. We were just making our plans when you came in. Right, Jill?

BARB: Oh, is that so!

ANN: Yeah, it is.

JILL: Excuse me. I think I can speak for myself. Barb, I won't be coming to the baptism. (ANN *looks triumphant.*) I do wish the best for Emily. But I don't think I would be comfortable. There is too much I guess I don't understand about it. (*To* ANN) And, Ann, I won't be going to church with you, either. I have a feeling I just wouldn't fit in. (*To both of them*) I thought I was interested in Christianity. I have admired you both individually and thought you both had a lot in common—things that I wanted for myself . . . now I'm not so sure. (*She starts to leave and then turns back.*) Oh, and by the way, in our house *(gestures to the doughnuts)* I like the ones with sprinkles—Eric likes to dunk his. But we both agree that we like doughnuts. In fact, we have doughnuts together every Sunday morning. See you later. *(She exits, leaving them both with doughnut on their faces.)*

The end

Discussion starters:

1. Is this play really about baptism? What is it about?

2. What do you think Jill thinks of Christians after this discussion?

3. How do our denominational and doctrinal differences help or hinder the process of evangelism?

They All Want Something

Themes: Grace extended—grace rejected, family, aging

Scripture: Matthew 22:1-14

Cast:

MARIE: *the loving and concerned daughter of Ethel; married and expecting a child*

ETHEL: *a lonely, bitter woman; suspicious and distrustful of everyone, including her daughter*

Props:

Magazine
Purse
Bouquet of flowers
Letter
Other pieces of mail

Running Time: 5 minutes

(*A living room in an upper-class home, extravagant, yet with a sterile coldness. There are two stuffed chairs, a coffee table, and a trash can.* ETHEL *is seated onstage, reading a magazine.*)

MARIE (*enters from outside carrying a bouquet of flowers*): Hello, Mom.

ETHEL (*surprised*): How did you get in here?

MARIE: The door was open, so I let myself in. How are you today?

ETHEL: Who wants to know?

MARIE: I want to know, Mother. Do you see anyone else here? So, how are we doing?

ETHEL: I don't know how we are. We seem to be alive.

MARIE: Mother, I was simply asking you how you were doing.

ETHEL: It was your Uncle Edward who sent you, wasn't it? He was always up to something.

MARIE: Nobody sent me, Mother. I came on my own. I wanted to see you.

ETHEL: What for?

MARIE: Because you're my mother. I wanted to . . .

ETHEL *(picks up her purse):* How much money do you need?

MARIE: I don't need money, Mother.

ETHEL: You can't borrow the car. I'm having a new alarm system installed. The newest on the market. The old one has been around so long all the thieves have probably figured it out by now.

MARIE: I don't need the car, mine is working just fine.

ETHEL *(noticing MARIE's pregnant state):* When's the baby due again?

MARIE: Middle of December. Mother, Jason and I would like to know . . .

ETHEL: No, I won't be able to help out after the baby is born. It's a very busy time of year, you know.

MARIE: I wasn't asking you to, Mom. Jason has already arranged for time off from work. I was going to ask if you would like to be with Jason and me for the delivery. We would like you to—if you want to be there . . . to see your grandchild enter this world?

ETHEL: Oh, I don't think I would like that.

MARIE *(giving up):* Fine. I brought your mail in for you. Looks like you got a letter from Walter Bonner.

ETHEL: Mind your own business. Spying on me.

MARIE: Mother! Really, I was just reading the return address. *(Sigh)* So, how is Walter?

ETHEL *(throws letter away unopened):* I don't know, and I don't want to know. He has been a real pest since your father died. Sends me cards and flowers. Probably after my money or this house or something.

MARIE: Mom! Walter has been a friend of the family for years. I'm sure he just wants to let you know he cares.

ETHEL: He was your father's friend, not mine. I have always questioned his motives. He was too cozy with your father.

MARIE: Mother! He was Dad's best friend. He helped Dad get his business going. How can you say such a thing? *(Reaches down and retrieves the letter from the trash)*

ETHEL *(looking at her mail, throws each piece away unopened, mumbling to herself):* This one wants money. This one wants me to volunteer. They all want something from me.

MARIE *(opening the letter):* Mother, this is an invitation from Walter. He is having a wing at the hospital dedicated in memory of Dad. He wants you to come, of course.

ETHEL (grabs letter from her): I told you to mind your own business. Who does he think he is? He should have consulted me about all this.

MARIE: Maybe he tried. If you throw all your mail away unopened, how would you know?

ETHEL: Well, I have a phone, you know.

MARIE: Sure. You have a phone, but you never answer it. I have called here day and night. All I get is your answering machine with your message: "This is Ethel. Whatever you are selling, I don't want it." You have the machine set on announce only, so I can't even leave a message. The only way I get to see you is if I drop in unannounced.

ETHEL: Well, he can just forget it. I am not going to any dedication. In fact, if I have my way, there won't be a dedication.

MARIE: Why, Mother? This is a great honor. Dad gave so much to others. He was an institution at that hospital. He deserves this recognition.

ETHEL: Just an excuse for everyone to line up at my door asking me for something. They expect me to be like him. They expect too much. They took all they are going to get. They are not getting their hands on any more. It is mine now.

MARIE: Oh, sure, it is yours legally. But Dad earned it. He loved you and provided you with all you would ever need for the rest of your life. Dad was very generous. He gave to others; they didn't take from him. That is why Walter is having the dedication. He wants to give something back to Dad for all he has given to others. You were special to Dad, and Walter respects that. You should feel honored. He doesn't want anything from you. Besides, he is a very wealthy man in his own right. What could he possibly want from you? (Long pause) Except possibly your friendship.

ETHEL: No. He wants something. They all want something.

MARIE (giving up again): Well, I think I'll be going. Good-bye, Mother.

ETHEL: Wait. What was it you wanted?

MARIE: Nothing, Mother. I didn't come here for something. I came here to see you, to see how you were doing.

ETHEL: Oh. I am fine. (A look) That's all?

MARIE: Well, there is one more thing. Would you . . . ?

ETHEL: I knew it! There is always something. Well, what is it?

MARIE: Would you like to have lunch with me? My treat!

ETHEL: Oh. No, thank you. I am busy today.

MARIE *(defeated):* I figured. Good-bye, Mother. *(Walks over and kisses her on the cheek and hands her the flowers)*

ETHEL: Good-bye, Marie. (MARIE *exits. After she leaves the stage,* ETHEL *looks at the flowers then tosses them in the trash can.)* She wants something. They all want something. *(Exits)*

The end

Discussion starters:

1. Why do you think it is so hard for Ethel to accept the generosity of others?

2. Have you ever reached out to someone only to have your kindness rejected? How does that make you feel?

3. Read Matthew 22:1-14. Give examples of how we can be guilty of rejecting God's gifts to us.

To Have and to Hold?

Theme: Divorce, resolving conflict, communication

Scripture: 1 Corinthians 7

Cast:
    LARRY: *an unhappily married man*
    ELLEN: *an unhappily married woman*

Props:
    Coffee cup
    Miscellaneous dishes
    Newspaper
    Purse
    Checkbook
    Briefcase

Running Time: 5 minutes

(At the breakfast table. LARRY is finishing his morning coffee and reading the paper. He is about to leave for work, briefcase at his side. He is detached and uninvolved. ELLEN is beginning to clear the table. She focuses on LARRY and clearly has something on her mind.)

LARRY *(not looking at her):* Ellen, where is the checkbook?

ELLEN: It's right here. *(Gets it from her purse and hands it to him)* Larry, why don't we take the kids and go to the coast this weekend? We could use the time away.

LARRY: I have to go to Seattle on business. Did you forget? The Mitsakato merger?

ELLEN: Oh. Yes, I did.

LARRY: Besides, I don't think we can afford any extras right now. *(Looking at the checkbook)* What happened here? I remember transferring $150 out of savings on Friday. I was going to buy some new tires. Now, where did it go?

ELLEN: The kids. *(Sarcastically)* You do remember—we have two. They needed some new clothes for going back to school.

LARRY: Well, why didn't you charge it?

ELLEN: Ditto on your tires. Besides, I thought we were over the limit on Visa. I seem to remember your telling me we were having a moratorium on our charge cards.

LARRY: Oh, forget it! Though I don't know what the big deal is about "back-to-school clothes," not with the way kids dress today. "Anything goes," and on our kids it seems the further gone the better.

ELLEN: No, let's not forget it. You do this all the time. You are so selfish! Whenever you want something, the money is always there. But when the kids or I need something, we never seem to have enough.

LARRY: Let's not have this discussion again. I'm not in the mood—OK?

ELLEN: Yeah, right, not in the mood for a lot of things lately. *(Thinks a minute)* The Miskato *(mispronouncing it)* merger—

LARRY: Mitsakato.

ELLEN: Whatever. *(Suspiciously)* Is that the one that Sheila Bergman is working on?

LARRY: Uh . . . yeah. Who told you that?

ELLEN: Is she going to Seattle too?

LARRY: Uh . . . *(evasively)* I don't know.

ELLEN: You don't know? How could you not know?

LARRY: OK, yeah, yeah, she's going too. So what?

ELLEN: So what! You're seeing her again, aren't you?

LARRY: Ellen, let's not get into that.

ELLEN: Just answer my question. You are seeing her, aren't you?

LARRY: Sure, I see her every day—at work.

ELLEN: All of these late nights this last month—you were with her, weren't you?

LARRY: I was working on the merger.

ELLEN: With her?

LARRY: All right, yes, with her. She *is* my partner on the project.

ELLEN: I can't believe it. After all we went through with your "little affair" before. You are actually seeing her again. You probably requested her as your partner. *(Sees by his reaction that it is true)* Oh, Larry, how could you?

LARRY: Look, it's nothing. *(Switches to attack)* But even if it were—what do you expect? At least she appreciates me. She doesn't attack me every time I turn around, like some people I know. Look, we are just working together. That's all.

ELLEN: You expect me to believe that.

LARRY (*on his feet*): I don't care what you believe. I've had it up to here with you and your suspicions.

ELLEN: What do you expect? You're the one that had the affair.

LARRY (*grabs briefcase and throws newspaper into it*): I don't want to have this discussion. (*Pause*) Look, I've thought about this for a long time. I just don't think it's going to work. Ellen, I want a divorce.

ELLEN (*hit out of the blue*): Wha . . .

LARRY: You should know that I've already seen a lawyer. Let's be realistic. You know it's not working between us. I hate to say this but, I just don't love you anymore—I'm sorry.

ELLEN: Larry, don't . . .

LARRY: I think it's best I leave now. (*He starts to leave; she reaches for him.*)

ELLEN: Larry, no, we have to talk . . .

LARRY (*pulling away*): It's best this way. I'm sorry, Ellen. I'll get my things later. (*Exits*)

ELLEN (*calling after him, hysterical*): Larry, no! What am I supposed to do? What about the kids? Larry! Larry! Oh, God, no . . . no . . . now what . . . what do I do? Oh, God, no! (*Sinks into chair and breaks down in sobs*)

The end

Discussion starters:

1. Who is to blame for the problems in this marriage?

2. Is there any hope for this marriage?

3. What steps should a married couple take to prevent this type of situation from happening?

Why Wait?

Themes: Sexual responsibility, parenting, dating

Scripture: Titus 2:6-8

Cast:

JASON MARKHAM: *a teenager struggling to do the "right" thing*
NED MARKHAM: *Jason's father, struggling to find the "right" answers*

Props:

Calculator
Papers
Pen
Basketball

Running Time: 5 minutes

(The den in the home of the Markham family. There is a desk and easy chair in the room. NED is seated at the desk doing work from the office, a calculator and papers strewn about. JASON enters, carrying a basketball and sits in the easy chair.)

JASON: Dad, do you have a minute?

NED *(working, not looking up):* Huh? . . . Oh, yeah, sure.

JASON: You know that Amy and I have been going out quite a bit.

NED: Uh, huh . . .

JASON: We really like each other.

NED *(still working):* That's good . . . she is very nice, I'm sure.

JASON *(can't believe NED said that):* I'm sure? *(Shakes his head)* Dad, we're getting serious.

NED *(suddenly has his attention):* Serious? What do you mean?

JASON: I mean we are getting serious. We love each other.

NED: Wait a minute. Hold the fort. You . . . uh, love each other? You're still in high school.

JASON: So?

NED: So—you are a bit young to be in love.

JASON: Dad, we've been dating for two months.

NED (*sarcastically*): Oh, well. What was I thinking? Then I guess you are ready. When are you getting married?

JASON: Married? I didn't say anything about marriage.

NED: You said you were getting serious.

JASON: Yeah, we are. But we're not talking about marriage.

NED: Well, that's good. Your mother will be relieved. (*Starts to go back to his work*)

JASON (*not sure how to ask this question*): When you and Mom were dating . . . did you wait?

NED: Wait? Yeah we waited, if you want to call it that. We were engaged for a whole year before we got married.

JASON: I don't mean that. I mean did you wait . . . you know . . . before you . . .

NED (*suddenly seeing, uncomfortable*): Uh . . . Why don't you go talk to your mother about this?

JASON: I did.

NED: And what did she say?

JASON: To come and talk to you.

NED: Oh, great. (*Awkwardly*) You mean, did we wait . . . wait, uh (*stalling*) . . . for what?

JASON (*blurts it out*): Did you sleep together—before you were married?

NED (*stunned, not liking this conversation, takes off his glasses and rubs his nose*): Uh . . . son, there are some questions a child just doesn't ask his parents.

JASON: You always said I could ask you anything.

NED: Yeah, but not that . . . that's different.

JASON: How? (*A hard look*) You did, didn't you?

NED (*defensively*): Why do you jump to that conclusion?

JASON: Because if you didn't, you would tell me right out.

NED (*heavy sigh; he has been had and he knows it*): Look, it is really none of your business. Why do you want to know?

JASON: It's OK, Dad. Never mind. (*Starts to leave*)

NED (*sudden flash of insight*): Jason, hold it. Does this have anything to do with Amy?

JASON: Well . . . yeah . . . kinda.

NED (*awkward again*): Are you two . . . uh . . . you know?

JASON: Are we sexually active?

NED: Yeah . . . like that.

JASON (*matter-of-fact*): No.

NED (*whew*): Good!

JASON: Not yet.

NED (*double take*): What do you mean, "not yet"?

JASON: Not yet, that's what I mean.

NED: But you are thinking about . . . it . . . becoming . . . uh . . . active.

JASON: Oh, yeah, Dad. We think about it a lot. (NED *swallows hard.*) A whole lot.

NED: Well, you know it is best to wait till marriage.

JASON: Yeah, I know. (*Tries again*) Did you and Mom wait?

NED: That is irrelevant!

JASON: I don't think so. I hear you say "wait," but then I hear kids at school say "do it." I know it's overused, but it seems that the phrase "everybody's doin' it" really applies, Dad. Even in health class the assumption is that we're already "doin' it"; they just want to make sure that we are "doin' it right"—the safe sex thing. It's hard to know what's right. Why should I wait?

NED: Son, you are very young—too young to be experimenting with sex.

JASON: It is not an experiment, Dad. Besides, I'm 17! And Amy is special. We really do love each other.

NED: Son, there is more to it than that. There can be some bad consequences. Especially today with sexually transmitted diseases and unwanted pregnancies—it is better to wait.

JASON: Yeah, yeah, I've heard all of that. One more time—did you and Mom wait?

NED: Why is that so important to you?

JASON: Because (*sigh*) deep down inside I want to wait; it feels like the right thing to do, but . . .

NED: That's good, Son! Trust that feeling.

JASON: But there is so much pressure. And then when we are alone . . . together . . . I just thought that if I knew that you and Mom waited . . . well, maybe that could help me make up my mind.

NED: Son, your mother and I had been going together for a very long time.

JASON *(not letting him off the hook)*: Did you wait?

NED: We were very much in love.

JASON: So are Amy and I. Did you wait?

NED: We knew we were going to get married, Jason.

JASON *(not a question)*: So you didn't wait.

NED: No—we didn't wait.

JASON *(disappointed)*: Thanks for being honest. *(Gets up to leave)*

NED: Son, wait. There is something else I want to say. *(Pause)* You know how you said that deep down inside you want to wait—that it feels right?

JASON: Yeah.

NED *(takes his time)*: Your mom and I felt that way too. In fact, we still do. We both have regretted the fact that we didn't wait. Oh, we tried to say to ourselves that it didn't matter—but it did. What we did was wrong, Son, and we knew it. You think about that before you and Amy see each other again. Will you promise me that?

JASON: OK, Dad. I promise.

(JASON exits. NED watches him go, then closes his eyes in a pained look and what could be the beginnings of a prayer.)

The end

Discussion starters:

1. Is it appropriate for Jason to ask his parents such an intimate question?

2. Is there a better way for Ned to have handled this situation?

3. In light of his past, does Ned have a right to expect Jason to do differently than he did?

The Letter

Themes: Suicide, grieving, forgiving self

Scripture: Romans 12:9-21

Cast:
NEIL: *a father trying to cope with a terrible loss*

Props:
Notepad
Pen

Running Time: 5 minutes

Note: This play deals with the suicide of a teenager. If played properly, the audience should not figure out that the son is dead until the end of the play. This makes the impact of the play even stronger. While the play is emotional, the actor playing Neil needs to use restraint in his emotions so as not to foreshadow the ending. While the actor "reads" the letter, it is important that he not focus just on the letter. His eyes need to come off the page as he reflects, thus letting the audience in on his thoughts.

(As the scene opens we see NEIL *onstage behind a desk. He is just finishing a letter. He looks it over, nods slowly in approval and begins to speak.)*

NEIL *(to himself):* There. It's done. *(A pause, then he starts reading the letter.)*
Dear Son,

It's your birthday today and I felt a need to write you this letter. It has taken a long time for me to be able to answer your letter. So much has happened lately that I want to share with you. I wish you were here so we could share in person.

Your mother is doing very well. This last year has, of course, been a struggle—not having you around. Yesterday we went shopping, you know your mother and shopping; she shops and I warm the bench outside the store. We passed by a computer store and naturally I started thinking of you. In fact, I considered buying you this new game, then I remembered. Oh well, probably would have been obsolete before I got it home . . . things change so fast these days.

Anyway, what I want to tell you is that I have made what I feel is an important discovery. You see, I have come to understand that I have really failed you as a father. I have always loved you but had a hard time showing it, let alone saying it. My way of showing it was to give you the freedom to do whatever you wanted, even when you were very young. I was always, as they say, "permissive" with you, even when I wanted to say no. I was afraid that I would somehow lose your love. I mistakenly thought

39

that if I said yes to everything, you would love me back. I gave you every-thing you asked for, hoping for your love in return.

Part of my reasoning was out of rebellion toward my own parents. They were so strict and I vowed never to be like them. Instead of finding a happy medium, your mom and I went to the other extreme. Now I see how wrong that was. Our permissiveness was interpreted by you as not caring. Even though we did not approve of the crowd you chose as friends, the parties, and as we found out later, the drugs—it took us a long time to come to grips with that one—we chose not to intervene. But I did care; I was just afraid. Afraid I would drive you away. In the end I did just that.

But I have to tell you, Mom and I have learned a lot lately. We are in counseling and have even started going to church. I know, I know, we used to go when you were very young but stopped when you complained . . . our mistake again. Anyway, we are going now and I am learning more about being a father as I learn more about God, our Heavenly Father. I re-alize now, more clearly, the mistakes I made with you. Mom and I have become Christians and . . . I know you probably won't believe it . . . but it has made a big difference in our lives.

I guess what I want to say—need to say, really—in response to your letter, is that we don't blame you, at least not totally, for what you did. We have to share in the blame. It has taken a long time for me to come to grips with all that has happened, but through Christ I have found forgiveness. I have also forgiven you for your part. I only wish I could have yours. I guess it is too late for that.

It saddens me that you will never read this letter, but somehow it has helped me to write it just the same. Happy birthday, Son.

I love you.

Dad

(He thinks a minute then begins to write again.)

P.S. Mom and I bought flowers for your grave today. I wanted to get that computer game, but Mom insisted . . . *(breaking down in tears)* maybe next year . . .

(He carefully folds the letter and places it in an envelope that he then places in his Bible. He hugs the Bible to his chest as the lights fade.)

The end

Discussion starters:

1. Can you speculate as to why the son committed suicide?

2. Is the guilt the father feels justified?

3. What words of comfort or advice (if any) would you give this father?

The New Wardrobe

A mime for one actor

Themes: Righteous living, redemption, new life

Scripture: Colossians 3:1-10

Cast:
   MIME: *not happy, a worldly type, in need of "new clothes"; can be male or female*

Running Time: 6 minutes

Note: While this can be done in total silence, a musical score will greatly enhance the impact of this piece.

(This play is a spin-off of the Marcel Marceaux routine "The Mask." The stage is bare, but the scene to be established is a home with a bed, closet, phone, and front door. There are no props, as everything is imaginary.)

MIME wakes up to the imagined sound of an alarm clock. He gives a yawn and gets out of bed. He is sad, in the doldrums. He goes over to the closet and opens the door. He slides several hangers aside, trying to decide what to wear today. He is not very enthusiastic about any of his choices. For the sake of simplicity and decency, we will make all the garments jackets. He lets us know that the clothes are badly worn and out of date.

He selects the first jacket. He turns his back to the audience as he puts it on. He immediately becomes the socialite. Cigarette in one hand, cocktail glass in the other. A party scene ensues. He mimes conversation while getting progressively drunk. After establishing a certain level of obnoxiousness, he finally staggers and turns away from audience, takes off the jacket and hangs it up. He is sad again.

He then selects a second jacket, turns his back to audience, as before, and puts it on. This time he becomes the greedy executive type. As he faces the audience, he exudes arrogance. He adjusts his tie, then flips a coin in the air. Image is everything. Pulls a wad of bills from his pocket and begins to count them. He picks up the phone, dials, and then begins chewing someone out over the line. He goes on a tirade. He is angry, yelling, and working himself into a frenzy. He is not getting his way. Finally he hangs up. He abruptly turns away from the audience and takes off his jacket and hangs it up. Sad again.

He selects a third jacket. Again turns his back to the audience and puts it on. This time he becomes pure sensuality—as sexy as possible within the boundaries of good taste. He looks over his shoulder at the audience, gives a "come hither" look and winks. Turns around very much the stud and struts around "flaunting his stuff," so to speak. He motions for someone to join him on the dance floor. He does a few steps with his imaginary partner, ending with a dip. Then he takes the partner into his arms, turns his back to the audi-

41

ence, and we see the "one person embrace" with his own hands exploring his back. Finally he takes off the jacket and resumes sadness.

(Note: If a female is playing the MIME, *then adapt above section, making her more of a seductress.)*

There is a knock at the door. He goes to the door, opens it. It is a deliveryman with a package for him. He is surprised, questions the deliveryman, then takes package, thanks him, waves good-bye, and kicks door closed with his foot.

After closing the door, he double-checks the address and tears open the package. It is a gift. Excitedly he opens the box to discover a brand-new jacket. He is in awe. This one is bright and glowing, causing him to squint. He slowly and hesitantly reaches out and touches it. He loves it—it is perfect. He picks it up with great care, turns his back to the audience and puts on the jacket. When he turns around this time, he is a new person we have not seen before. He is glowing and warm, and almost floating. There is a smile so big it almost breaks his face. He then looks heavenward, hugs himself, brings his hands over his heart and then up in such a way that we get the feeling he has his heart in his hands. He is changed. He offers his hands up as an act of worship—in effect, giving his heart to God.

He then almost floats over to the closet and grabs the other jackets. He holds them at arm's length—they are suddenly repulsive to him. He opens the door and tosses them out. He brushes off his hands as the lights dim and we come to . . .

The end

Discussion starters:

1. Identify and discuss what each "outfit" the character wore represented.

2. Are there similar "outfits" in our own closets that need to be thrown out?

3. As represented in the play, what are the characteristics of the new wardrobe that gave the character meaning and purpose?

The Ungrateful Smedds

Themes: Thanksgiving, appreciation, family

Scripture: Colossians 3:15-17

Cast:
    DADDY SMEDD: *stern and eccentric, with no sense of humor*
    MOMMY SMEDD: *proper and efficient and also eccentric*
    JOEY SMEDD: *a very serious and sheltered young man*
    SUZIE SMEDD: *a teenager, on the verge of rebellion*
    GRACE FULLER: *the only normal person, friendly and outgoing*

Props:
    Newspaper
    Textbook
    Coffee
    Doughnuts
    Wallet
    Brochure
    Purse

Running Time: 7 minutes

Note: This sketch is like something you might see on *Saturday Night Live*. The characters should be played bigger than life, to the point of absurd. Have fun!

(A living room in middle-class America. There is a sofa, easy chair, and coffee table. As the play opens, JOEY is seated on floor at the coffee table doing some homework.)

DAD *(enters, crosses to easy chair looking for the paper, speaking sternly):* Son, where is the newspaper?

JOEY: I'm going out to get it now, Dad. *(Runs off)*

DAD *(calling after him):* That is the proper thing to do, you know. I expect you to do that each morning. *(Sits)*

JOEY *(offstage):* It'll be right there in a sec.

DAD: Oh, wife. It is Saturday. As usual, I should like to drink my coffee in the living room while I read the paper.

43

MOM *(offstage):* Yes, my husband. It is almost done brewing. I will bring it to you when it is finished.

DAD: I expect that you will, just as you have in the past.

JOEY: Here is your paper, Father, as expected.

DAD: Yes, open it and place the sports section on top.

JOEY: Yes, Father.

SUZIE *(entering):* Dad, I am going to the mall with Sarah today. I have not received my allowance yet. Would you give it to me now?

DAD: Did you do the required tasks and receive no deductions this week?

MOM *(entering with coffee):* Here is your coffee, as expected.

JOEY: No, she did not, Dad. It was her turn to do the dishes on Thursday night and she skipped out. I had to do them. She was supposed to trade, but she didn't do them for me at all this week.

MOM: That is true. How can we ever take you for granted when you do not do what is expected?

DAD: It is important to learn these things so that we can all depend on each other. You shouldn't need to be told or constantly reminded.

SUZIE: You are right. I expect that you will make a deduction from my allowance. It is, after all, payment for what I am expected to do, and if I don't carry out my responsibilities, then I should not expect to be paid.

DAD: You are learning. *(Looks in his wallet; doesn't want to part with his cash)* Wife, would you give the money to our daughter?

MOM: Yes, my husband. I took it for granted that you would say this to me. I have already set the money aside. *(Exits)*

DAD: I expected that. You know me so well. Suzie, I expect that you will drive carefully, and as usual fill the car with gas before you return.

SUZIE: I have always done this, Father. You did not need to say it.

DAD: I have not reached the point where I can take you for granted yet, young lady. Until I do, you can expect me to say such things to you.

SUZIE: Yes, Father. I expect you will.

MOM *(entering with tray of doughnuts):* Well, everybody, here is our usual Saturday morning breakfast, doughnuts—as expected.

JOEY: Did you remember to get me my jelly-filled, chocolate-covered raised doughnut with sprinkles?

MOM: Now, what do you think, Joey? Did you even need to ask?

JOEY: I guess not. I forgot. I know I should have taken you for granted.

MOM: Yes, you should have.

DAD: Let us pray. *(Adopts proper posture and waits for the family to do likewise)* God, Thou hast done what we expected this week. Thou hast provided for our needs. We expect that Thou will continue to do the same next week. Thou already knows that Thou art a great and mighty God, so we don't need to tell Thou that. We say this prayer in the name we take for granted, Jesus Christ, Amen.

MOM: Everyone, help yourselves.

(SFX: doorbell rings.)

SUZIE: I'll get it. *(Exits)*

MOM: Yes, you should. *(To* DAD*)* Who could that be? I am not expecting anybody. Are you?

DAD: No, I'm not.

SUZIE *(enters with* GRACE FULLER*)*: They're in here, Mrs. Fuller.

(From this point on, all the SMEDDS *twitch or jerk in some comical way, every time* GRACE *says the words "thanks" or "thank you." At first* GRACE *is oblivious to this, then gradually she begins to notice and is finally distracted by these strange reactions. Likewise, the* SMEDDS *grow increasingly irritated with her repeated use of the dreaded "T" word.)*

GRACE: Thank you, Suzie. *(Family twitches)*

SUZIE: Mom and Dad, this is Grace Fuller from the church down the street. Mrs. Fuller, these are my parents, Mr. and Mrs. Smedd, and my brother, Joey. *(They shake hands.)*

DAD: Have a seat, Mrs. Fuller.

GRACE: Thank you. *(More twitches)*

MOM: We were in the middle of our usual Saturday morning routine of doughnuts and coffee. Would you like a doughnut?

GRACE: No, thank you. *(Twitches)* I can only stay a minute. Suzie visited our church with her friend Sarah last week. I just wanted to thank you *(twitches)* for visiting, Suzie. I also wanted to invite all of you to come and visit on Sunday.

DAD: To tell you the truth, we have considered it. We don't go to a church right now—but we are Christians, you know.

GRACE: Well, good. You know, this Sunday we are having our special Thanksgiving *(twitches)* service. We want to express our thanks *(twitches)* and gratitude for all that God has done. It is so easy to take Him for granted.

We need to remember to give Him thanks *(twitches)* for all the many blessings He has given us.

DAD: Well, we shall certainly give it some thought.

SUZIE: Mrs. Fuller, tell my mother about the women's study that is coming up.

GRACE: Oh, right. Thank you *(twitches)* for reminding me, Suzie. The women are beginning a study called "The Thankful Heart." *(Twitches)* It is all about how we can change our whole outlook on life if we can learn to thank God *(twitches)* for everything that comes our way—good or bad.

MOM: Oh, that sounds . . . interesting.

GRACE: Of course, our church has programs for all ages. Joey, I have a son about your age. He thinks there are a few too many girls in his Sunday School class. He would be so thankful *(twitches)* to have another boy involved. They have a lot of activities planned for the remainder of the year.

JOEY: Really. That sounds cool. Thank— *(Stops himself as the family all twitch and then stare at him in shock.)* . . . I mean, it is good to know that.

GRACE *(she notices this, is uncomfortable and wants to leave):* Here, let me leave this brochure with you. *(Hands it to* DAD*)* It tells about the church and all the various programs. *(Stands to leave)* Well, I mustn't stay. Thank you *(twitches)* for giving me these few minutes to share with you.

DAD: It was good of you to stop by.

MOM: Maybe we will see you on Sunday.

GRACE: I hope so. Thanks again. *(Twitches)* Good-bye, Suzie. Nice to meet you, Joey. *(She exits.)*

SUZIE: Bye.

JOEY: Bye.

DAD: Well, that was certainly . . . unexpected.

MOM: What an unusual woman.

DAD: She certainly knows how to use the "T" word, doesn't she?

JOEY: That Sunday School class sounds pretty awesome.

SUZIE: Well, I'd better go. I was supposed to pick up Sarah 10 minutes ago. May I have my allowance now?

MOM *(hands it to her):* There you go. I think that is the expected amount.

SUZIE: Yes, it is. Thank you. *(They all twitch,* SUZIE *puts her hand to her mouth, then they all smile sheepishly, except* DAD *who glares at her as she exits.)*

MOM: Here, have another doughnut, Joey.

JOEY *(for the first time):* Thank you. *(Twitches and giggles)*

MOM: You're welcome. *(Twitches and more giggles from* MOM *and* JOEY *as* DAD *glares disapprovingly.)*

The end

Discussion starters:

1. What is this family's main problem?

2. What are the consequences of taking people for granted?

3. Are there people that you feel take you for granted? That you take for granted?

What's It Worth?

Themes: Christmas, giving vs. receiving, values, purpose

Scripture: John 3:16; Hebrews 1:14

Cast:
> GABE: *by all appearances, a homeless, mysterious, and strangely helpful individual; perhaps he is more than he appears to be*
> MR. PERKINS: *a businessman, in a hurry; late for work*
> KAREN: *a teenager; the responsible, more mature type*
> MEGAN: *another teenager; Karen's younger sister; the irresponsible, immature type*
> CHRIS: *another homeless person (man or woman)*
> MARY: *a wife, mother, and homemaker at the end of her rope; depressed and frustrated*

Props:
> Newspaper
> Briefcase
> Money
> Books
> Two sack lunches

Running Time: 10 minutes

(A bus stop outside a shopping mall. There is a park bench, garbage can, and bus stop sign. Christmas music is playing in the background. GABE is sitting on the park bench, pulling newspaper, which he has been using for warmth, out of his clothing. As he pulls each section out, he places it neatly next to him on the bench. A businessman, MR. PERKINS, with briefcase in hand, approaches. He warily regards GABE, walks behind him to the far end of bench, then notices the paper. He picks it up and leafs through it, noticing there is no business section, which is what he wants. He grumbles when he can't find it and begins to look around for it; eventually looking in the garbage can. His back is to GABE, who takes the business section from his coat and places it on the bench. MR. PERKINS turns and sees the paper, grabs it, then does a double take, as he wonders where it came from. GABE appears to be minding his own business. MR. PERKINS suddenly realizes it might be GABE's paper and speaks to him.)

PERKINS: Oh . . . uh . . . is this your paper?

GABE: That's awright.

PERKINS: I'm sorry. I thought someone left it here.

GABE: They did—about 6:00 this morning.

PERKINS: Well, here, let me pay you for it.

GABE: Nah! I just borrowed it myself. You go ahead. Did you find the section you wanted? *(Starts to see if he has another in his clothes)*

PERKINS: Yes, I was just looking for the business section. I've been looking for a paper all morning. The machine back there was out. I left the house before ours arrived.

GABE: Well, help yourself. Oh, here *(pulls out another section)*, this section goes with it.

PERKINS: Well, thanks. Here, take this. *(Holding out a dollar)*

GABE: That's not necessary. They only cost a quarter, and I didn't buy that one noway. Merry Christmas. *(Indicating paper is a gift)*

PERKINS: You look like you could *(stops himself)* . . . just take it. It's worth it to me. I can't get through the day without the stock market report. *(Throws dollar at GABE)* Ah, here's my bus. Uh, thanks again . . . Merry Christmas. *(He exits.)*

(GABE *watches him go, then picks up the dollar, pockets it, and smiles. He hears voices and moves behind bench and sits on the ground beside garbage can. Two teenage girls,* KAREN *and* MEGAN, *enter on their way to school. They have books and sack lunches in hand, are in conversation and don't notice* GABE.)

KAREN: I've found an awesome gift for Mom, a gorgeous scarf. It's just perfect! It's got all the right colors and everything!

MEGAN *(sitting on bench):* That's great, Karen. Say, have you seen those new sweaters at Macy's? I asked Mom and Dad to buy me one for Christmas, but I can't wait. They're so cool. I almost have enough saved to buy it now.

KAREN *(sits beside her):* What are you getting Mom for Christmas?

MEGAN: Nothing . . . maybe a card.

KAREN: A card! That's it? A card?

MEGAN: Yeah. I don't have money for anything.

KAREN: You would if you didn't buy that sweater.

MEGAN: Hey, that's my allowance I've been saving!

KAREN: So what? Isn't it worth your allowance to buy something for Mom? I mean, Christmas only comes once a year, you know.

MEGAN: Come on, Karen. Dad will get her something nice and put our names on it too—he always does.

KAREN: That's not the same, Megan, and you know it. You're old enough now to do something on your own. Think of all the things Mom does for us all year. Look, why don't you go in with me on the scarf? If you helped, we could even get some earrings to match. It could be a gift from both of us—and Mom would really love it. *(Starts counting her money)* I only need a couple more dollars to get the scarf, and if you help we can get the earrings for about $10 or $15. What do you say?

MEGAN *(getting up):* Forget it, Karen. I've had my eye on that sweater for a long time. Stop trying to make me feel guilty. Mom knows I love her. She won't be expecting a gift from me, anyway. Come on—let's go or we'll be late for school. (MEGAN *leaves.* KAREN *watches her go then starts to leave when* GABE *gets up and moves toward her.)*

GABE: Excuse me, Miss.

KAREN *(startled, regards him nervously):* Huh?

GABE *(holds out the dollar):* I think this is yours.

KAREN *(looks down at her money):* Oh . . . well . . . *(Unsure)* Thank you. *(Reaches out and takes it)* I must have dropped it.

GABE: Say, I couldn't help overhearing your conversation with your sister. I think your mother will like that scarf. And if I were you, I'd go ahead and look at some earrings. She'll come around. You gave her something to think about.

KAREN: You really think so?

GABE: Yep.

KAREN: I hope so. She can be so selfish sometimes.

GABE: We all can. But people can change. *(A knowing look)* I'll bet you have.

KAREN: Yeah . . . yeah, I have. *(Looks at him as if to ask "how did you know?")* I better go. Thank you. *(Indicating the money, she starts to leave. Stops, fingers the dollar, wondering if she really did drop it.)* I'm not sure this is mine.

GABE: It's yours. Keep it. Now you had better hurry or you'll be late.

KAREN: You're right, thanks! *(Exits)*

GABE: Merry Christmas.

(Turns and realizes that KAREN *left her lunch on the bench. Picks it up to give it to her, but she is long gone. He opens the sack and looks into it. Smiles and nods as he sits down.* CHRIS *comes on; he is hungry and looking for food. He goes to the garbage can and starts digging.* GABE *sees him [her] and begins laying out the food as if he were having a picnic.* CHRIS *notices this and looks longingly at the food. As* GABE *finishes the "table setting" he walks over and escorts* CHRIS *to the bench as if he were a maître d'.* CHRIS *begins to stuff himself, then feels bad and offers* GABE *some food.* GABE *declines, perfectly content to see* CHRIS *well-fed. He stuffs some food in clothing and gives* GABE *an awkward hug and then exits.* GABE *looks around whistling or humming "Angels We Have Heard on High" and wondering who's next. He begins pick-*

ing up garbage left strewn about by CHRIS. *He dusts off the bench as* MARY *enters carrying a shopping bag and newspaper. She sits and looks off, really depressed.*)

GABE (*sitting at other end of bench*): Good morning.

MARY (*gives him an uncomfortable glance*): Well, at least the morning part is accurate.

GABE: Not good, huh? (*Shakes her head*) Sorry.

MARY: You think it's good? (*Looks at him, thinking "obviously not"*)

GABE: Yep!

MARY: Why? I mean you look . . . uh . . . I mean, well you know . . . sorry.

GABE: Don't be. You've heard the saying "looks can be deceiving"? (*Smiles*)

MARY: Well, yes, but . . . never mind.

GABE: Why is this only a morning and not a good morning?

MARY: You wouldn't be interested in my problems. You probably have enough of your own.

GABE: Not really. And I would be interested.

MARY: I don't know. It's almost Christmas, and I just don't have the spirit this year.

GABE: Just what "spirit" might that be?

MARY: You know, the joy, excitement—the spirit! You know.

GABE: Ah, yes, I certainly do. But do you?

MARY: What?

GABE: Know the Spirit of Christmas? What is Christmas . . . to you?

MARY: Pressure—too many things to do. Family conflicts—his family, my family. Not enough money—not enough time. Shopping, long lines, traffic jams. Kids saying "I want this" and "I want that." I'm about at the end of my rope. I'm not sure it's worth it.

GABE: No, probably not—without the Spirit.

MARY: What do you mean?

GABE: Well, if Christmas is all those things you mentioned, why bother . . . ?

MARY: Well, that's exactly . . .

GABE: Without the Spirit.

MARY: You keep saying that.

GABE: You said it first. You said you didn't have the spirit this year.

MARY: Yeah, I guess I did.

GABE: You know what Christmas is, don't you? I mean, why it's celebrated.

MARY: Well, of course—I mean the birth of Christ, and all.

GABE: Especially the all!

MARY: But it's so complicated today. When I was a kid, it was so simple. Christmas was giving and getting presents, family traditions—a real celebration!

GABE: Sounds like you need to recapture some of that celebration. Especially the part about giving. It's the key to the real Spirit question, you know.

MARY *(defeated):* I'm not sure I do anymore.

GABE: Sure you do! Think about it. It starts out "For God so loved the world that he . . . caused us pressure, family conflicts, not enough money and traffic jams." *(She laughs; he smiles.)*

MARY: I know the verse . . . "that he gave his only begotten Son, that whosoever believeth in him should not perish, but have everlasting life."

GABE: Very good. Now, for Christmas the key word there is *gave*. You think about that, and I bet you recapture that Spirit that has been eluding you.

MARY: Yeah, you may be right. *(She thinks about it for a moment, then checks her watch.)* Well, I must be going. *(Starts to leave)* Uh . . . thank you . . . uh . . . I don't know your name.

GABE: Gabe.

MARY: Mine is Mary.

GABE: Mary, I like that. Merry Christmas, Mary.

MARY: Merry Christmas, Gabe! Bye! *(Exits)*

GABE: See you later! Oh, wait—you forgot your paper! *(She is gone.)* Oh, well. *(He looks heavenward.)* Thank you! *(He takes the paper and begins unfolding it as he stuffs it back into his clothing and hums or sings "Joy to the World.")*

The end

Discussion starters:

1. Who is Gabe and what is he trying to accomplish by his actions?

2. Define in your own words what is "the real Spirit of Christmas."

3. What do each of us do to help keep the proper focus during the Christmas season?

Celebration City

A readers theatre presentation

Theme: Unity and fellowship in the body, evangelism, self-centeredness

Scripture: Matthew 7:24-29

Cast:
>NARRATOR 1: *can be male or female*
>NARRATOR 2: *can be male or female*
>JONATHAN DOUGH: *an enterprising and self-centered young man*
>MR. DUNKEN: *Jane's father and resident of Celebration City*
>JANE DOUGH: *Jonathan's sweetheart, but also her own person*
>MRS. DUNKEN: *Jane's mother*
>CHORUS

Props:
>Scripts
>Tissues

Running Time: 15 minutes

Note: This is a great play for a banquet or special event—entertainment with a message. While it is true that this is a "reading," it should be well rehearsed to the point that the script is needed only for cueing. Readers should come off the script when they are speaking as much as possible. Pacing and timing are very important in the delivery.

(Cast could be either standing or seated on stools. Scripts may be held or rest on music stands. From SR to SL: NARRATOR 1, MRS. DUNKEN, JANE, JONATHAN, MR. DUNKEN, NARRATOR 2. All cast members double as the chorus unless the chorus lines come in the midst of their dialogues. As the scene opens, the cast can file onto stage with classical music playing in the background. Dressing as formally as possible and looking very "serious" helps set up the humor even better.)

NARRATOR 1: Once upon a time, there was a happy place called Celebration City. The people who lived there lived their lives in a constant state of Celebration.

NARRATOR 2: Anyone visiting the city would hear laughter . . .

CHORUS: Ha, ha, ha!

NARRATOR 2: . . . and singing.

CHORUS: La, la, la, la, la, la, la, la. *(To the tune of "London Bridge")*

NARRATOR 2: They would see people helping each other.

MR. DUNKEN: Let me give you a hand with that.

JONATHAN: Thank you very much.

NARRATOR 2: Good deeds abounded.

NARRATOR 1: This is not to say there were never any problems or moments of sadness—for there were. But in such times the residents would rally around each other and support each other in such a way, that even these times eventually resulted in . . .

CHORUS: Ta-da!

NARRATOR 1: . . . Celebration!

NARRATOR 2: For, you see, the residents of Celebration City knew the secret of their happiness—which wasn't really a secret at all.

NARRATORS 1 and 2: They knew their Creator . . .

CHORUS: Ahhh!

NARRATORS 1 and 2: . . . the source of their joy!

NARRATOR 1: Now Celebration City was located on the Coast of the Sea of Fears . . .

CHORUS: Oooh . . .

NARRATOR 1: . . . and in the middle of the Sea of Fears was an island called the Island of Self.

CHORUS: Self, self, self, self, self . . .

NARRATOR 1: The only resident of the Island of Self was a man named Jonathan Dough.

NARRATOR 2: Jonathan Dough was a baker and was well known throughout Celebration City for a pastry he called a raised bread pastry but which the residents nicknamed—the "doughnut."

NARRATOR 1: A name he never endorsed, as the pastry looked nothing like a nut, and secretly he feared that the nut referred to him rather than the pastry.

NARRATOR 2: Jonathan was a good man—

NARRATOR 1: Well, at least he wasn't a bad man.

NARRATOR 2: He worked hard.

NARRATOR 1: He was a decent citizen.

NARRATOR 2: He considered himself a citizen of Celebration City, although he never spent much time there. When he had business to conduct, he would row his boat to the city.

CHORUS: Row, row, row . . .

NARRATOR 2: He would occasionally be seen at some of the community Celebrations, and while he somewhat enjoyed these, they were often what he considered a . . .

NARRATOR 1 (*sounding bored*): . . . major inconvenience.

CHORUS (*Loud "raspberry" [put tongue between lips and blow]; after the raspberry the cast members take tissues and pat their lips dry.*)

NARRATOR 1: But these visits were good for business, so he endured them.

NARRATOR 2: Jonathan enjoyed many things about Celebration City; however, he was only a passing acquaintance with the Creator of the joy.

NARRATOR 1: Jonathan, from all appearances, was a man who had it "all together," as the expression goes. After all, he was a respected businessman who had his own private island. Whenever Jonathan was in public, he put on a big smile and conducted himself in a manner that conformed to those around him.

CHORUS (*All smiles*)

NARRATOR 2: But when Jonathan was alone on his island his smile faded and his "all together" appearance began to fall apart.

JONATHAN: Day after day I do my work. I make my pastry for the citizens of Celebration City. But I feel my life is beginning to resemble these raised bread pastries. We both have a hole . . .

CHORUS: Whoosh! (*Air-out-of-balloon sound*)

JONATHAN: . . . in the middle. There must be something I can do to fill up this hole.

NARRATOR 1: One day, while Jonathan was delivering his pastries in Celebration City, a chance encounter occurred that would drastically alter his perspective.

JONATHAN: Pastry for sale! The finest pastry this side of Plentiful Valley. Get your raised bread pastry here!

MR. DUNKEN: Good day to you, Master Dough.

JONATHAN: Greetings to you, Dunken.

MR. DUNKEN: I will have 10 of those doughnuts, Jonathan.

JONATHAN: They are not doughnuts, Dunken. I call them raised bread pastry.

MR. DUNKEN: If you say so.

JONATHAN: I sell them by the dozen now. A dozen is the same price as 10.

MR. DUNKEN: A dozen then. Say, have you given any thought to my offer to open a shop here in the city? I would be interested in investing in such a venture. The whole town is nuts about your dough- *(stops himself)* . . . uh, your raised bread pastry.

JONATHAN: I know, and I am considering it. Mr. Winchell made me a proposal the other day as well.

MR. DUNKEN: Oh, he did? What did he offer you?

JONATHAN: No offer yet. Just said he was interested, like you.

MR. DUNKEN: Think about it, Jonathan. We could call it Dunken's Doughnuts!

JONATHAN *(doesn't like it):* Oh, please!

MR. DUNKEN: Oh, all right, but if you ask me, it has a nice ring to it. A lot better than Dough's Raised Bread Pastries.

JANE: Papa! Papa! Oh excuse me, I . . . oh . . . uh *(Sees* JONATHAN *for the first time as he sees her for the first time. It is love at first sight.)*

MR. DUNKEN: Oh, Jane. *(To* JONATHAN*)* Jonathan, I would like you to meet my daughter, Jane. Jane, this is Jonathan Dough. He makes the doughnuts—er, the raised bread pastry that you like so much.

JANE: Hello.

JONATHAN: Uh . . . hi. Would you like a raisednut doughbread?

JANE *(Giggles)*

JONATHAN *(embarrassed):* I mean a doughraised nutbread?

JANE: I'm not sure what that is. But I would love a doughnut.

JONATHAN: Absotively . . . I mean posolutely. Here, have a doughnut.

JANE: Why, thank you.

NARRATOR 2: And from that moment on, raised bread pastry was now and forever called . . .

NARRATOR 1: The doughnut.

NARRATORS 1 and 2: Ah, what joy!

NARRATOR 2: Jonathan and Jane were in love.

JONATHAN and JANE: Ahhh!

NARRATOR 2: They spent every moment they could together.

JONATHAN and JANE: Ohhh.

NARRATOR 2: Jonathan was no longer alone and lonely.

JONATHAN and JANE: Hmmm.

NARRATOR 2: A few months later they were married* in one of the biggest Celebrations that Celebration City had ever seen.

*(CHORUS *begins humming "Here Comes the Bride" on word "married" above. Then a loud "yippee" at the end.*)

JONATHAN and JANE *(Loud kissing sound)*

NARRATOR 1: They went on a glorious honeymoon in the State of Bliss. Jonathan had found something to fill that hole in the middle of his life. It seemed that life could not have been happier.

NARRATOR 2: They settled on the Island of Self, and in the beginning, Jonathan and Jane Dough shared everything with each other. There were no secrets.

NARRATOR 1: However, Jonathan learned that Jane took longer in the bathroom than she ought.

NARRATOR 2: And Jane learned that Jonathan spent more hours baking and selling doughnuts than he ought.

NARRATOR 1: He thought she should check with him before spending money.

NARRATOR 2: She thought he was too "tight" when it came to money.

NARRATOR 1: But they would talk about these little differences and things would be all right . . .

NARRATOR 2: . . . for a while.

NARRATOR 1: However, there came a day when they stopped talking about those little things that bothered them. They reasoned that they had learned to accept each other "as is," so to speak.

NARRATOR 2: They didn't need to talk about it; in fact, they found very little to talk about any more. While they were together every day . . .

NARRATOR 1: . . . they were also very far apart. Life became boring, and before long Jonathan noticed that empty feeling . . . that hole . . .

CHORUS: Whoosh!

NARRATOR 1: . . . was back again.

NARRATOR 2: And Jane, who had never experienced this empty feeling when she lived in Celebration City, was discovering a hole . . .

CHORUS: Whoosh!

NARRATOR 1: . . . in her life as well.

JANE: Jonathan, why don't we go into the Celebration City in the morning. I should like to attend the weekly Celebration. It has been some time since I have been in the presence of the Creator of the joy. Shall we go?

JONATHAN: You can if you like, but I have too much work to do.

JANE: You always have work to do. Let us go together; the work can wait.

JONATHAN: I can't. It's time to make the doughnuts. (*Said like the commercial*) Why don't you go with some of your friends?

JANE: What friends? Since I have moved onto the Island of Self, I have seen very little of my friends. We go to Celebration City only when we "have to." We never invite anyone to come here for a visit—not that they would want to, anyway. This place is so boring.

JONATHAN: Oh, don't start that *boring thing* again. I have put a lot into this place. And besides, we have each other.

JANE (*unenthusiastically*): Yeah, we have each other. Good night. I am going to bed.

JONATHAN: Good night, dear.

JANE: Try not to wake me when you come to bed. Last night you . . .

JONATHAN: Yes, dear. Good night!

NARRATOR 1: Meanwhile, in Celebration City, life was grand.

CHORUS: Ha, ha, ha and la, la, la, la.

NARRATOR 1: The residents of the city were experiencing the joy of their Creator and their community like never before.

NARRATOR 2: And, while it was grand for them, it only served to make Jonathan and Jane even more aware of the void in their own lives. They felt they had nothing to celebrate. They had no joy for themselves, for others, and most importantly, for the Creator of the joy.

NARRATOR 1: This, of course, did not escape the notice of Mr. and Mrs. Dunken. They were especially concerned about Jane, as she had once been so full of the joy.

MRS. DUNKEN: Jane, we miss you. We never see you at the Celebrations anymore. The only time we see Jonathan is when he makes his deliveries. Even then, he doesn't stay long. What is wrong? Have we done something to offend you and Jonathan?

JANE: No, it is not you. (*Crying, dabs eyes with tissue*) Oh, Mother, I am so sad these days. When Jonathan and I were first married we were so happy. We thought nothing could ever happen to make us sad again.

MRS. DUNKEN (*comforting her*): Here, here, child.

JANE: But now we have lost our joy. I don't know if I can ever get it back. We hardly talk anymore. I never see my family and my friends. I don't know what to do.

MR. DUNKEN: You must leave the Island of Self. You must move to Celebration City.

JANE: Jonathan will not consider it. I think he is afraid of something.

MRS. DUNKEN: What could he be afraid of?

JANE: I have asked him about moving here, but he says he needs his privacy. He has put so much into developing the Island of Self—he says he could never abandon it. The thought of losing the island terrifies him. But he is so unhappy. I love him, you understand.

MR. DUNKEN: Of course, you do. I don't know if Jonathan has heard the latest news, but the island is not what he thinks it is. He thinks he has a great treasure there, but the land is all sand and is getting smaller each year. In a few years, it will be all but covered by the Sea of Fears.

JANE: What can we do? His heart is hard. He will not listen to me.

MR. DUNKEN: Come, let us talk to the Creator of the joy. Only He knows how to soften a hardened heart.

NARRATOR 1: So the Dunkens and Jane, along with several in the community, took their case to the Creator of the joy.

CHORUS: Hallelujah! *(To the tune of the "Hallelujah Chorus")*

NARRATOR 2: I wish I could say that here is where a happy ending comes. But alas, it is not . . .

CHORUS *(pouting):* Awhhh.

NARRATOR 1: . . . at least not yet.

CHORUS: Ohhh?

NARRATOR 1: As is so often the case in dealing with a hardened heart, something terrible had to happen before Jonathan was willing to soften his heart. You see, for Jonathan to change, he first had to get to know the Creator of the joy. While Jonathan had been introduced to Him, he did not know Him.

NARRATOR 2: Jonathan had been invited to the Creator's house, but he always had a reason for being unable to attend. And the thought of inviting the Creator of the joy to visit him, on his island, had never even entered his mind.

NARRATOR 1: Now the Creator of the joy was not one to force himself on another, although, to those who knew Him it was hard to fathom why anyone would choose not to know Him. He would reside only where He was invited. It would appear there would be no hope for Jonathan, were it not for the fact that so many of the residents of Celebration City had petitioned the Creator on Jonathan and Jane's behalf.

CHORUS: Please, oh please, oh please, oh please . . .

NARRATOR 2: The Creator of the joy found it almost impossible to resist the sincere requests of the citizens of Celebration City. Especially when those requests were many, and on behalf of someone else and not themselves.

NARRATOR 1: I do not know if the Creator of the joy "caused it," or if it was just "happenstance," but one day while Jane was visiting in Celebration City, and while Jonathan remained on the Island of Self, there came a terrible storm.

CHORUS (*Storm sounds—wind blowing, fingernails tapping on folders for "rain" sound*)

NARRATOR 2: It rained so hard and the wind blew so fiercely that it was impossible to travel across the Sea of Fears for almost three days.

NARRATOR 2: To Celebration City this was a minor inconvenience as it was built on Rock, and the water just ran into the Sea of Fears. But not so for the Island of Self.

CHORUS: Self, self, self, self . . .

NARRATOR 2: It turned out that what Mr. Dunken had said about the island was correct. It was, indeed, all sand, and it was sinking. At the end of the three days the island had all but disappeared.

NARRATOR 1: And so had Jonathan Dough.

NARRATOR 2: Jane and the Dunkens were very distraught.

DUNKENS: Ohhh! (*Distraught sounds*)

NARRATOR 2: Mr. Dunken set out with a search party to see if he could find Jonathan.

CHORUS: Row, row, row.

NARRATOR 2: In the distance were several pieces of floating debris. They hoped he would still be alive, clinging to what little remained of the Island of Self.

CHORUS: Self, self, self, self . . .

JONATHAN: Help! Help! Somebody help! . . . How could this happen? . . . I thought I had everything. I thought I had all I hoped for. Self was not at all what it was reported to be. All my hope was built on sinking sand. How could I have been so stupid? . . . how? . . . how? . . . how? . . .

NARRATOR 1: Clinging to a piece of wood, Jonathan drifted off into a state of semiconsciousness. He dreamed. In his dream he saw all the people of Celebration City in the midst of a Giant Celebration. All the people were so happy.

CHORUS: Ha, ha, ha and la, la, la!

NARRATOR 1: He wanted that happiness for himself. He saw the Dunkens—and he saw Jane. He called out to them . . .

JONATHAN: Dunkens!

NARRATOR 1: . . . but no one heard him. He tried to get closer and called again.

JONATHAN: Jane!

NARRATOR 1: But still no one heard him—no one saw him. He tried standing in front of people, but they seemed to look right through him. He followed their gaze.

NARRATOR 2: In the middle of the crowd was a throne and on the throne was a Man. He was the Creator of the joy. Suddenly, the Creator turned and looked at Jonathan. The Creator smiled, and then abruptly extended His arm, hurling something at him. Jonathan cowered in fear and screamed.

JONATHAN: AHHH!

NARRATOR 2: This was the end—he knew it. The Creator of the joy was going to kill him. He took one more look at the object . . .

NARRATOR 1: It . . . was . . . a doughnut! A large white, powdered doughnut was coming right at his head.

MR. DUNKEN: There he is!

JONATHAN: Why?! . . . He is going to kill me with a doughnut . . .

MR. DUNKEN: Grab ahold, son!

JONATHAN: No! . . . not with a doughnut! No! . . .

MR. DUNKEN: It is not a doughnut, Son, it is a lifesaver. Grab the lifesaver! You will be all right! . . . That a boy!

NARRATOR 2: Yes, indeed, Jonathan was rescued from the Sea of Fears!

CHORUS: Hurrah!

NARRATOR 2: . . . and the Island of Self. He was brought safely back to Celebration City and was reunited with Jane.

JONATHAN and JANE (Loud kiss sound)

NARRATOR 2: And one of the first things she did was to introduce him personally to the Creator of the joy.

CHORUS: Hallelujah!

NARRATOR 1: Mr. Dunken was all too happy to help Jonathan get reestablished in Celebration City, and the first-ever Dunken Doughnuts was opened in a few short weeks.

MR. DUNKEN: Oh, Jonathan, it's time to make the doughnuts!

NARRATOR 2: Now that Jonathan was a resident of Celebration City, he learned a new and more meaningful way of life. He became intimately acquainted with the Creator of the joy and discovered the wondrous fulfillment of being more than just an acquaintance with the other residents of Celebration City.

NARRATOR 1: His life with Jane was no longer boring. And, yes, they did live happily ever after . . .

NARRATOR 2: . . . and on to eternity as well.

NARRATORS 1 and 2: The end!

(Optional music plays while cast exits.)

The end

Discussion starters:

1. In what ways are you like Jonathan Dough?

2. Identify the things that kept Jonathan from wanting to be a part of Celebration City.

3. What role did Jane and Mr. and Mrs. Dunken play in Jonathan's "salvation" from the Sea of Fears?